R
RECIPES

Compiled by
Freya Trotman

*Favourite dishes of
Britain's kings and queens
with illustrations of the
royal palaces and houses.*

SALMON

Royal Recipes – an introduction

The challenge of compiling recipes from the royal households and courts is one similar to reducing a stock when cooking, in this case to make them fit cohesively into a compact book! There was also an issue with foods which are no longer in vogue, or those which are impossible to source. Lampreys may have been Henry I's fish dish of choice in the 12th century, but might pose more of a challenge to find now on the fish counter in most supermarkets, although some do stock them! Likewise, swans regularly graced the tables at royal banquets, but they are the property of the monarch, and it remains a criminal offence to take or harm one of these beautiful birds.

Many of the recipes, particularly those in the first few centuries after the Norman Conquest, would have originally been from the French kitchens. Over the next few hundred years when the French and the Anglo-Saxon cuisines integrated, what then occurred would, in modern times, be described as "fusion" cooking.

The Norman's brought their rabbits from the Continent, and no doubt became accustomed to our more strongly flavoured native hare. Equally, we introduced them to the delights such as samphire from the marshland coast, which nowadays is considered a delicacy.

The other main difference between our modern recipes and those of the past is the use of sweet and savoury foods commonly used together. A prime example being the humble mince pie, much enjoyed at Christmas, but which in its original form would have contained minced meat along with the fruit and suet!

Even the names of our meats as we know them now fell under the influence of the newly spoken French language. Mutton was from the French "mouton", and beef from the French "boeuf". Sheep and cow are not words we use to describe the meat on our tables. Indeed, to this day, menus for the royal households are still predominantly written in French!

From the first century, royal households were very mobile. The kings and queens, and their courts travelled as a massive entourage. Partly to dispense justice and settle disputes, but also to spread the immense cost of keeping the courtly personel fed and watered. The expense could be offset by expecting the unfortunate host to foot the bill! It also meant that in the days prior to any means of reliable communication, a royal visit allowed the commoners to see the monarchy in action, and of course, it served as a timely reminder to any would be troublesome nobility to toe the line; or else.... a cripplingly expensive second visit could follow with alacrity.

Not only did our eating habits change with the arrival of the Normans, but so did our manners! Cutlery, as we know it, consisted only of an eating knife, and a spoon. Most of the noble houses ate off trenchers, from the Old French "tranchier", meaning to cut. A carver would cut thick square slices of bread as platters and the meal would be eaten off these. Each course would be served on a new slice and when they were removed afterwards, they became the servant's portion, soaked as they were, in the remains of the master's meal. Others were given as alms to the poor.

These trenchers were the forerunners to our plates and placemats. Also, because the trenchers were given to the poor, whose meal consisted of the trencher itself (and who were unlikely to have had any form of cutlery); it became customary to only break the bread. A tradition we still observe today when eating bread with a meal. Bread was also served separately with the meal, and again was always broken, as it would have been for Communion. The Normans had also imported a stricter observance of religious practice along with their eating habits, requiring that there were many more days where meat would not be served!

Many of the recipes were obviously passed on by word of mouth, rather than being written down. The first known written recipe book was in the Plantagenet reign of Henry II and was the work of Alexander of Neckham at some time around 1170! Most of the recipes in this book therefore date from Victorian and Edwardian times. Many modern royal favourites are, thanks to chefs such as Tschumi and Roussin, far better documented. I hope you will find this compilation informative and the recipes enjoyable.

Index

Cover pictures *front:* Buckingham Palace, London   *back:* Windsor Castle
Title page: St. James's Palace, London
Page four: Holyrood Palace, Edinburgh

Printed and Published by Dorrigo, Manchester, England © Copyright

Venison with Frumenty

I could not compile a selection of royal recipes without the inclusion of venison. This was always the most jealously guarded of royal meats, and the penalties for killing any of the King's deer were dire indeed, ranging from being blinded, losing your hand, to being hanged or deported. Some of these laws were not repealed until 1823! The traditional dish to serve with venison has always been frumenty, a dish which is no longer common, even though venison is now readily (and legally) available!

INGREDIENTS
4 good sized venison steaks cut from the loin   Cracked mixed colour peppercorns   Sea salt   Good quality olive oil
1 garlic clove   4 tbs. port   4 fl.oz. good beef stock   4 fresh apricots   2 oz. fresh cranberries
FRUMENTY: 4 oz. kibbled wheat   14 fl.oz. full cream milk or single cream
1 oz. dried fruit sultanas, cranberries or dried apricots
1 beaten egg yolk   2 tsp. honey   2 tsp. powdered cinnamon   ½ tsp. ground all spice   Salt

METHOD
First make the frumenty. Soak the kibbled wheat in water overnight in a warm place so that the wheat softens. Next day drain off the wheat and boil gently in the milk or cream for 25 minutes, adding the dried fruit and then simmer over a very low heat for a further 40 minutes. Allow to cool, then beat the egg yolk with the honey and spices, and add to the wheat and milk. Season to taste with the salt. This can stand for the time it takes for the venison to be prepared. For the venison, stone and chop the apricots (discard the stones) and lightly crush the cranberries to allow the juice to release from the fruit. Halve the garlic clove and gently sautée in 2 tablespoons of olive oil in a heavy-based frying pan. Remove garlic clove and discard, but retaining the oil in the pan. Coat the venison steaks in the crushed peppercorns and sea salt. Heat the oil back up and pan fry the steaks on high for 4 minutes on each side to brown, then cook for about 12 minutes more slowly whilst you prepare the sauce. Mix together in a small saucepan the crushed cranberries, beef stock, chopped apricots and port, heat through to poach the fruit and allow the liquid to reduce slightly. When the steaks are cooked allow them to relax away from the heat for 2 minutes before slicing in long strips. The meat should be slightly pink. Serve with the frumenty, green beans and the fruity sauce.

Chicken Pilaff

This was a particular favourite of Queen Alexandra (born 1844, died 1925). It bears little resemblance to its spicier Middle Eastern roots, so I can only assume she prefered this plainer version.

INGREDIENTS
**1 medium chicken cleaned and dressed   ½ pint white wine   1 pint of water   1 bouquet garni   1 oz. butter
1 small onion   4 oz. mushrooms   8 oz. long grain rice
SUPREME SAUCE TO SERVE: 1 oz. butter   1 oz. plain flour
⅓ pint good chicken stock reserved from cooking the chicken   Egg yolk   2 tbs. cream   1 tbs. finely chopped fresh parsley**

METHOD
Pre-heat the oven to 350°F, gas mark 5. Place the chicken in a large casserole dish and add the white wine, water and bouquet garni and cook slowly for about an hour and a half. Remove from oven and drain stock into a jug, removing bouquet garni and skimming off the fat. Finely chop the onion and sautée in half the butter in a large saucepan until light golden brown. Add rice and fry for about 2 minutes. To this then add a pint of the chicken stock and simmer for about half an hour until the stock is absorbed. Slice the chicken once it has rested and set aside in the hot oven, covering it with foil. In a frying pan sautée the mushrooms in the remainder of the butter, but do not let them break up. Leave until the rice is cooked. To make the sauce supreme, melt in a saucepan the butter and blend in the flour until smooth. Slowly add the remaining reserved chicken stock and stir to make a smooth sauce. Add the finely chopped fresh parsley and simmer for five minutes. Beat the egg yolk with the cream and add to the sauce very last thing. Remove the chicken from the oven. Lay the rice on a serving dish, place the chicken on top and pour over the sauce, using the mushrooms to garnish. Season well and serve immediately. Accompanying dish should be duchesse potatoes.

Blancmange

Nowadays we regard blancmange as a sweetened custard often flavoured with fruit, but originally it was a savoury dish, and came to Britain with the Norman Conquest, hence its French name, and would have contained rice, meat, almonds and herbs. By medieval times, it was a combination dish of sweet and savoury elements, gradually becoming a wholly fruit-flavoured custard by Georgian times. Queen Victoria (born 1819, died 1901) regarded it as a great favourite, partly in deference to Prince Albert's delicate stomach. In this recipe I have retained the original ground almonds which give it a lovely texture along with the rose petals which deliver such a delicate flavour.

INGREDIENTS
6 gelatine leaves   1 pint whole milk   6 oz. caster sugar   1 tsp. rose water (don't be tempted to add a bit more, with rose water "less is definitely more"!)   ½ pint double cream   3 oz. ground almonds   A tiny amount of cochineal Ground nut oil   Twenty fresh rose petals with green parts at base of each petal removed as they are bitter

METHOD
Lightly brush a 1¾ pint or 1 litre mould with ground nut oil. Silicon rose moulds are ideal as an alternative and are very decorative. Cut gelatin into strips and cover with cold water in a bowl. Soak for 5 mintues then drain and place in a large mixing bowl. Stir the ground almonds into a little of the milk and then add to the rest before bringing it slowly to the boil. Pour milk and almonds over the gelatin and stir to dissolve. Add sugar and stir again to dissolve. Add the cream and rose water. Add a couple of drops of cochineal, but this is only intended to delicately colour the dish, not turn it fuschia pink! If you want to add the rose petals to the dish itself lightly chop them and add, alternatively they can be sprinkled on before serving. Place mould in fridge covered with cling film and allow to set for several hours.

To serve, remove the cling film, dip the mould into a bowl of hot water for a few seconds and with a plate over the top of the mould carefully turn over to allow the pudding to slide out onto the plate. Decorate with with further rose petals either fresh or crystalised.

Baron of Beef

Henry VIII (born 1491, died 1547) is alleged to have named this dish. As a renowned gourmand who loved his food, he had enjoyed an evening's feasting on this particular meal. To show his approval he took his sword and dubbed the meat saying "Arise, Sir Loin" This cut of beef consists of two sirloins left uncut at the backbone.

INGREDIENTS

Two sirloins of about the same size, or ask your butcher to leave them uncut at the backbone for a true baron of beef.
Zest and juice of a lemon   A handful of caraway thyme   2 crushed garlic cloves   1 tsp. crushed black pepper   1 tbs. of olive oil
FOR THE GRAVY: Cornflour mixed with a little cold water   ½ pint beef stock, plus the meat juices   ½ pint well-flavoured red wine

METHOD

The night before cooking, put the zest of a lemon, a handful of caraway thyme, 2 crushed garlic cloves, a teaspoon of crushed black pepper, and a tablespoon of olive oil into a pestle and mortar, and grind together. Add the juice from the lemon and infuse in a small covered dish in the fridge overnight. Before beginning cooking the meat, allow the beef to reach room temperature for an hour. Dry the meat with paper towels and then rub all over with the marinade and allow to absorb the flavours for another half hour. Pre-heat the oven to 450°F or gas mark 8. Heat a large heavy skillet with two tablespoons of well-flavoured olive oil, and seal the meat for a couple of minutes on each side. Place the meat fat side uppermost on a rack over a roasting pan. Immediately reduce the oven to 325°F gas mark 3 or 4. Cook uncovered for 25 minutes per pound for "medium rare", and 30 minutes per pound for a "medium" cook. The baron of beef should be served just pink in the middle. Cooked any more fiercely will result in meat which is progressively tough. To test, push a skewer into one of the sirloins, when it is removed the juices which seep out should just be pink. Transfer the meat to a plate and form a foil tent around it, and allow it to rest for quarter of an hour. While the meat rests, make the red wine sauce. Use a fruity full bodied wine and mix with equal measures of stock, heating together in the roasting pan on the top of the stove. Do this gently to loosen all the crusted on meat juices and drippings at the bottom of the pan, scrape loose anything which is burned on. This gives the gravy a really good flavour. Thicken by mixing equal parts of cornflour in cold water in a separate container and then pouring it into the meat juices slowly whilst stirring continuously. Keep this warm whilst carving the meat and serving the vegetables and accompaniments, such as horseradish sauce, Yorkshire puddings and roasted potatoes.

Queen Alexandra's Poulet à la Danoise

Queen Alexandra (1844 to 1925) had a great influence on the Royal eating habits, bringing with her from her native Denmark many recipes which must have reminded her of home. This was one she greatly enjoyed and was adapted by chef Gabriel Tschumi for her.

INGREDIENTS

A medium chicken, which has been cleaned and dressed   4 oz. butter   Juice and zest of lemon   Freshly chopped parsley Sliced red onion   A large peeled sliced carrot   2 sticks celery chopped and sliced   1 bay leaf   Black pepper and salt ½ pint good chicken stock   ½ pint double cream

METHOD

Pre-heat the oven to 350°F or gas mark 4. Cream the butter and half the lemon juice together with all the zest, and the parsley. Place this inside the empty chicken cavity. In the bottom of large lidded casserole, put the carrot, celery, onion slices and bay leaf. Place this in the pre-heated oven. The juices from the chicken should be sufficient to cook it and retain its moistness. Cook for 1½ hours.

When it is cooked remove from the oven, drain the juices into a saucepan and joint the chicken laying it in the bottom of the casserole dish with the vegetables and return to the oven to keep hot. In the saucepan add the rest of the lemon juice to the juices and add the stock, once it has reached simmering add the cream and reduce the sauce until it thickens slightly. Cover the chicken pieces with the sauce and serve very hot with fresh vegetables and potatoes.

Buckingham Palace Mutton Pies

These were frequently made during the time of Queen Victoria (born 1819, died 1901), and were popular both above and below stairs, as it meant the staff could enjoy them cold when there had been a hot dish upstairs.

INGREDIENTS
Short crust pastry made with 6 oz. of flour   **Puff pastry made with 4 oz. of flour**   **1 medium egg (beaten)**
8 oz. sliced and diced cooked mutton   **A little olive oil**   **2 finely chopped shallots**   **Chopped parsley**   **Half a small carrot**
Half a small celery stick   **½ pint (300ml.) good beef stock**   **2 tsps. cornflour to thicken**   **3 tbs. red wine**
1 tbs. redcurrant jelly   **Salt and pepper to season**

METHOD
First make the sauce by heating the oil and frying the shallots, finely chopped carrot, and finely chopped celery over a low heat until they soften. Add the beef stock and parsley, cover the saucepan and simmer for 20 minutes. Mix the cornflour with the red wine, and pour into the stock. Stir in the redcurrant jelly. Leave to cool slightly.

Roll the shortcrust pastry out fairly thinly and cut out cirles to fit a fairly deep patty tin, and smaller circles of puff pastry, to make lids for the tartlets. Fill each pastry case with the diced mutton and then add about a tablespoon of stock to each one. Wet the top of each tart and cover with a pastry lid, making sure each one is well sealed. Make a hole as a steam vent in each and brush the top of each tart with beaten egg. Cook in a hot oven for about 25 minutes at 350°F or gas mark 4. Serve hot or cold. These make an ideal picnic dish.

Queen Alexandra's Pommes de Terre à la Danoise

Gabriel Tschumi, apart from his grander creations, used to make this simple dish for Queen Alexandra (born 1844, died 1925), and serve it with either variation of the egg dishes oeufs suzette or oeufs cardinal. Ideal for a light lunch or supper dish.

INGREDIENTS
4 large baking potatoes weighing about 8 oz. each   2 oz. butter   5 fl.oz. milk   4 tbs. cream   Salt and pepper

METHOD
Scrub, prick and bake a large potato in its jacket for each person. When cooked and the skins are crisp, slice a large section from the top, scoop out the inside of the potato and the top, discarding the "lid" of the potato. Sieve the potato flesh and make it into a purée with butter, milk, cream and season with pepper and salt. Keep hot in the oven whilst preparing either of the egg dishes.

OEUFS SUZETTE
Lay thin slices of ham on top of the potato, top with a layer of hot bechamel sauce, a poached egg, a second layer of sauce and sprinkle with grated mature Cheddar cheese. Put under a hot grill for a few minutes to brown. Serve whilst hot.

OEUFS CARDINAL
Lay shredded cooked lobster on top of the potato, top with a layer of hot bechamel sauce, a poached egg, a second layer of sauce and sprinkle with grated mature Cheddar cheese. put under a hot grill for a few minutes to brown. Serve whilst hot.

Duke of Cambridge Tart

This tart was originally called Duke of Cambridge pudding, and may have been named after Prince George (born 1819, died 1904), grandson of King George III, whom it is alleged began his career in the military at the tender age of nine, and remained a professional soldier all his life. Indeed, many of the Dukes of Cambridge have been military men. This tart is made and eaten cold, it is a lovely addition to a picnic.

INGREDIENTS
**Shortcrust pastry made with 6 oz. flour   1 oz. chopped peel   2 oz. chopped cherries
4 oz. raisins soaked overnight in a little sherry   3 oz. butter   3 oz. caster sugar   2 egg yolks   2 tbs. rum or brandy**

METHOD
Pre-heat the oven to 375°F or gas mark 5. Line a tin with the shortcrust pastry, sprinkle it with the chopped peel, and chopped cherries and soaked raisins. Melt the butter gently in a saucepan and stir in the caster sugar and add the egg yolks, remove from heat and cool slightly stirring all the time. Add the brandy or rum, pour carefully over the fruit in the tart and bake for 25 to 35 minutes in a pre-heated oven until golden brown. Serve cold with ice cream.

Windsor Castle Carrot Pudding

This recipe was another developed by Gabriel Tschumi. It makes a lovely moist pudding with lots of flavour, and not too sweet.

INGREDIENTS
5 oz. grated carrot   5 oz. plain flour   3 oz. chopped suet   2 oz. currants   2 oz. chopped raisins
3 oz. soft light brown sugar or caster sugar   Zest of a large orange   ¼ tsp. grated nutmeg   Large pinch salt
½ tsp. baking powder   1 beaten egg   A little milk if required to slacken the mixture   A large greased pudding basin

METHOD
Combine all the dry ingredients together and then add the egg, stirring to form a stiff mixture which is properly bound together. If it seems too stiff add a little milk to the ingredients. Put pudding mixture into the greased basin and cover with a layer of greased tin foil secured tightly around the basin. Steam steadily for 3 hours, without allowing the saucepan to boil dry. Serve with custard or crème fraiche.

Parmesan Cheese

This very simple dish was greatly enjoyed by both King George VI (born 1895, died 1952) and Winston Churchill. It is far removed from anything they might have sampled at banquets or grand dinners for visiting dignitaries.

INGREDIENTS
Stale white bread cut into fingers about half an inch thick   Top of the milk or single cream
Grated Parmesan, gruyère or Cheddar cheese   Salt and pepper   A buttered tin

METHOD
Soak the stale bread fingers in the cream, and then roll them in the cheese, pressing it into the bread so it sticks properly. Place the fingers onto the buttered tin and bake them in a hot oven pre-heated to 375°F or gas mark 5. Turn them after about 5 minutes or when they are golden brown, to cook the other side. The fingers should be crisp on the outside and creamy inside. Season to taste.

George V's Favourite Pancakes

King George V (born 1865, died 1936), apparently loved pancakes and these came from Tschumi's kitchen.

INGREDIENTS
4 oz. plain flour   1 oz. caster sugar   Pinch of salt   2 large eggs   One and a half tbs. thick cream
½ pint whole milk   ½ oz. melted butter   A little brandy   Clarified batter for frying   Lemon wedges   Caster sugar to serve

METHOD
Beat everything together for 10 minutes except the milk, brandy and melted butter, then add these and stir well. Allow the batter to stand for 2 to 3 hours.

In a heavy-based frying pan melt a small amount of clarified butter and then cover the base thinly with batter. When the pancake becomes loose, flip it over (with a spatula if you are not confident at tossing pancakes) and serve with caster sugar and lemon wedges. These will keep hot with a layer of greaseproof between each if you want to serve everyone together.

King Edward's Golden Brie Tart

The reign of King Edward I (born 1239, died 1307), saw several changes in the royal eating habits. Edward fought in the campaigns across the Scottish Borders, bringing home the Stone of Scone which has graced the Coronation Throne in Westminster Abbey for every coronation since. So it seems appropriate to include one of his dishes in this compilation. Whilst in Scotland, he tasted smoked haddock, and brought it back to the kitchens of England; in addition, Brie cheeses were imported for the first time from France. The saffron gives this tart its golden appearance. Gilded or endored food had been fashionable for many years, and generally speaking, the gaudier the dish the more impressive it was considered to be.

INGREDIENTS

YOU WILL NEED: 9 inch spring form flan tin or dish   Shortcrust pastry made with 8 oz. flour   ¼ pint single cream 3 eggs   4 oz. ripe Brie   4 oz. naturally smoked haddock left in large flakes; drained, skin and bones removed Pinch of cayenne pepper   Pinch of saffron strands   1 tbs. chopped chives

METHOD

Pre-heat the oven to 400°F or gas mark 6. Thinly roll out the pastry and line the tin or dish. Line with non-stick paper and fill case with baking beans and blind bake for about 10 minutes. Remove the paper and beans and cook for another 10 minutes. Allow case to cool completely before filling. Reduce oven temperature to 350°F or gas mark 5. Put the cream and saffron into a small saucepan and bring to the boil quickly to allow the saffron colour to infuse the cream. Turn the ring off and allow to stand for 5 minutes before pouring into a jug through a sieve to remove saffron. Cool for 10 minutes. Break up the Brie into pieces and put this and the smoked haddock flakes into the flan case and sprinkle on the chopped chives. Beat the eggs and cayenne into the cream and pour slowly into the pastry case. Put in the middle of the oven and cook for 30 to 35 minutes, until the tart is set and golden. Leave for 5 minutes before cutting if serving hot, or may be served cold with a green salad.

Mushrooms à la King

This dish is served either on a bed of noodles or rice for luncheon and was one of the favourites of King George V (born 1865, died 1936). He also had a penchant for mashed potatoes and insisted on them being served at all private meals! This dish serves two.

INGREDIENTS

2 oz. celery, finely sliced and cooked in a small saucepan of water for 5 minutes, and drained
1 large egg hard boiled, cooled, shelled and thinly sliced   1 oz. butter
½ lb. brown mushrooms, with stems removed and quartered
4 oz. dry weight rice or noodles
1 rounded tbs. flour   ½ pint single cream   Pinch of paprika   A few chopped black olives to garnish

METHOD

While rice or noodles are cooking, melt the butter in a frying pan and sautée the mushrooms for 5 minutes and then stir in the flour until blended, then pour in the cream slowly. Stir continuously adding the paprika. When sauce is smooth and boiling add the drained stewed celery. Make a ring with the cooked rice or noodles and top with the slices of egg. Pour mushrooms into the middle, garnish with olives and serve immediately.

Queen Mary's Birthday Cake

Judging from this birthday cake, Queen Mary (born 1867, died 1953), had a very sweet tooth. Serve in thin slices as it it very rich!

INGREDIENTS
8 egg yolks   2 egg whites   4 oz. caster sugar   3 oz. plain flour sifted twice   2 oz. butter melted
FOR THE CHOCOLATE GANACHE: 1 pint whipped cream   6 oz. caster sugar
1 lb. 2 oz. grated good quality dark chocolate   To decorate, crystalised flowers and angelica pieces

METHOD
Pre-heat the oven to 350°F or gas mark 4. Whisk the egg yolks and sugar together in a bowl over a pan of hot water for about 10 minutes until doubled in volume and very pale and thick like double cream. Carefully pour in the melted butter and fold into the mixture. Separately whisk the egg whites until they are standing in soft peaks, (use a spotlessly clean bowl for this, or they will not whip up), then fold these into the mixture, with a light hand. Sift the flour twice then carefully add to the mixture and again fold in very carefully so as not to reduce the volume of the sponge. Pour mixture into two Victoria sponge tins which have been lined with silicon parchment or greased greaseproof paper which has been lightly floured. Cook in the oven for about 30 minutes. Allow cakes to cool for a few minutes before turning out onto clean tea towels rather than a wire rack which will mark the light sponges. Cool fully before cutting each cake in half to make four layers.

For the ganache: Boil cream, sugar and grated chocolate in a heavy-based saucepan, stirring to combine ingredients, do not allow to burn. Remove from heat and allow to cool for an hour. Assemble the cake by filling each sponge layer with the ganache and then topping the cake with it as well. Decorate with crystalised flowers and angelica.

Princess Royal's Dessert

Princess Louise, Princess Royal and Duchess of Fife (born 1867, died 1931), was the third child and eldest daughter of Edward VII and Queen Alexandra. This is a very indulgent and sweet dessert, ideal for a dinner or lunch party. I imagine her guests would have been delighted if this was on the menu!

INGREDIENTS
FOR THE GENOISE: 3 eggs   3 oz. caster sugar   3 oz. plain flour   2 oz. melted butter
Vanilla or chocolate ice cream for cake filling
FOR THE CHOCOLATE SAUCE: 2 oz. good quality dark chocolate grated   2 oz. cocoa
8 oz. caster sugar   ½ pint boiling water

METHOD
Pre-heat the oven to 350°F or gas mark 4. To make the Genoise sponge, place the eggs in a large bowl with the sugar and whisk over hot water until the mixture is the thickness of whipped cream and has doubled in volume. Fold in the melted butter and flour which has been sifted twice. Do this very gently or some of the volume will be lost and a heavy sponge will result. Pour into Victoria sponge cake tins which have been lined with greased greaseproof paper which has been lightly floured, or silicon parchment and cook for 25 to 30 minutes. Leave to cool in the tins for a few minutes and then turn out onto a folded tea towel rather than a wire rack which will mark the light sponges.

For the chocolate sauce: Mix all the ingredients together in a saucepan and simmer together stirring constantly. This is a very quick sauce to make. Leave to stand for a few minutes whilst you sandwich the sponges together with a thick layer of ice cream. Serve with the hot sauce.

Sandringham House, Norfolk

Boar with Pear Confit

This was a popular meat with monarchs for hundreds of years. The pear confit complements the boar beautifully.

PEAR CONFIT INGREDIENTS

**4 large ripe but firm pears. (You can also use red crab apples if you prefer)   3 oz. finely chopped stem ginger
8 oz. stoned chopped dates   1 tsp. ground ginger   1 tsp. ground cinnamon   ¼ tsp. ground cloves   8 oz. soft light brown sugar
¼ pint (150ml.) sherry   ½ pint (300ml.) full bodied red wine   Zest of a lemon   6 tbs. apple or pear brandy**

PEAR CONFIT METHOD

Peel the pears and remove cores and stalks. Cut into medium-sized chunks. Put all ingredients (apart from the brandy) into an oven-proof casserole. Soak for 24 hours. Heat oven to 180°C gas mark 4, and put casserole dish into it immediately reducing the temperature to 120°C or gas mark 1 or 2. Cook the fruit for about 3 hours. Mixture should have a thick consistency depending on the fruit water content. If it is too thick, add a couple of tablespoons warmed sherry and add with the brandy, if too thin, mix a little arrowroot with the brandy and stir through. The confit should be served cold in a dish at the table, but it is equally good served warm.

**To feed 6 adults allow ½ lb. weight per person   3 lb. boned rolled loin boar   1 tsp. coarse salt and some ground black pepper
Marinade: 1 tbs. dried mustard   2 cloves garlic chopped   1 shallot chopped   Mixed finely chopped herbs consisting of sage,
thyme, rosemary, marjoram   2 bay leaves   10 juniper berries   1 tbs. recurrant jelly   ½ pint (300ml.) red wine
2 tbs. cider vinegar   2 tbs. honey   ½ pint (300ml.) strong chicken stock   2 tbs. olive oil   3 tbs. arrowroot**

METHOD

Mix all the marinade ingredients together in a saucepan and heat for about 5 minutes. Allow to cool completely. Wash and dry the meat and place in a large casserole dish. Pour over the marinade ensuring the meat is completely coated. Leave for 2 days, turning the meat a couple of times, covering all surfaces. At the end of this time remove the meat from the marinade and dry it well, rubbing in the salt and black pepper. Pre-heat the oven to 170°C gas mark 3 to 4. Sear the meat on all surfaces in a large heavy frying pan in the olive oil until golden brown. Drain the marinade from the large casserole dish into a saucepan, add most of the chicken stock, reserving a little of the stock to stir separately into the arrowroot. Heat the stock and marinade together and when boiling, add the arrowroot and rest of the stock. Put the browned meat back into the casserole dish and pour on the stock, cover with lid. Put into the oven. Cook very slowly for 2½ hours, basting twice. Remove and allow to rest before carving. Serve with roast potatoes and vegetables and the pear confit.

Tarte Bourdaloue

This is a classic pear and almond tart. Originally made by Coquelin, whose patisserie still exists on the Rue Bourdaloue in Paris, this version graced the royal dining table after being adapted by Charpentier. Traditionally, the pear slices should be arranged in a cross formation as the Rue Bourdaloue was itself named after a 17th century clergyman.

INGREDIENTS
You will need a 9 inch fluted loose-based flan tin
FOR THE PASTRY: 7 oz. plain flour   4 oz. butter   1 oz. icing sugar   1 large egg yolk   1 tbs. very cold water
FOR THE FILLING: ½ pint milk   ½ vanilla pod   1 tbs. sugar   1 egg yolk   1 tbs. cornflour
6 crushed amaretti biscuits   ½ tsp. almond essence   4 pears cooked, halved, and sliced in ¼ inch (or 5mm.) slices

METHOD
Rub the butter into the flour and icing sugar, until it resembles fine breadcrumbs. Add the egg yolk to the water and mix before adding it to the flour mixture. Bring the mixture together with your fingertips to make a ball of pastry. Chill for 15 minutes. Dust the base of the tin with flour and then lightly roll out the pastry. Rest for 15 more minutes and pre-heat the oven to 400°F or gas mark 6. Prick the base of the tarte and cover base with baking parchment and baking beans and cook for 15 minutes. Remove beans and paper and cook for another 10 minutes. Allow to cool for 15 minutes while you make the filling. First split the vanilla pod and scrape the seeds out into the milk. Bring the milk to the boil. Beat the egg yolk, almond essence, sugar and cornflour in a separate pan, and then slowly add the boiled milk, continuing to stir all the time. Put the mixture over a low heat stirring until it thickens, do not allow it to boil. Strain the custard and add the crushed amaretti biscuits. Cover the base of the pastry case with the custard and then add the sliced pears in a cross pattern. Fill the case with the rest of the custard, and put under a medium grill or in a very hot oven to brown for a few minutes. Serve hot or cold.

Bavarois au Chocolat

This dish was one of Queen Victoria's favourites and was once served to 1,900 guests at one of her garden parties. It was developed by Marie-Antoine Carême (born 1784, died 1823) who was undoubtedly a celebrity chef in his day. He was the most famous patissier and confectioner of his time and enjoyed the patronage of the royal families in Europe and Russia. He was chef de cuisine to the Prince Regent (born 1762, died 1830), later King George IV. He is generally credited with developing this dish, and it remained a royal favourite for generations to come.

INGREDIENTS
**1 pint milk   1 pint whipped cream   7 oz. icing sugar   8 sheets of gelatin
10 oz. dark good quality chocolate with minimum 70% cocoa solids   6 egg yolks**

METHOD
Cut up the gelatin sheets and put them into a basin covering them with cold water. Soak for at least 5 minutes before draining. Break up the chocolate into squares and put in a basin over warm water to melt slowly for about 10 minutes. When it has melted, add the egg yolks and icing sugar and mix them all together whilst the milk is brought to the boil in a saucepan. Pour milk slowly into the chocolate mixture whisking continuously to stop the eggs curdling. Whilst the mixture is still fairly warm, stir in the gelatin. Allow to cool for a short while before folding in the whipped cream, stirring until the mixture is uniform throughout. Pour into serving dish. Chill until completely set. Decorate with cream if desired and serve with petit fours.

Prince Albert's Pudding

Prince Albert (born 1819, died 1861), had a delicate digestion and much preferred plain food. Indeed, when he and Queen Victoria ate privately, it must have caused consternation for the chefs knowing that if Victoria disliked a dish she would grimace. This pudding must have been an acceptable compromise. Sweet enough to tempt, but plain enough to be enjoyed.

INGREDIENTS

**14 oz. prunes   1 pint water   3 oz. white breadcrumbs   2 oz. caster sugar   4 oz. butter   ¼ tsp. baking powder
2 large eggs separated   Zest and juice of a lemon   1½ oz. plain flour   2 oz. soft light brown sugar
FOR THE SAUCE: 1 rounded tbs. arrowroot   1 pint prune liquid   2 oz. light soft brown sugar   4 tbs. rum**

METHOD

Soak the prunes in water for about 5 minutes before bringing them to simmering point in a saucepan with the half the lemon zest, all the lemon juice and light soft brown sugar (from the pudding ingredients). When they are tender and plumped up, remove from the heat and drain liquid into a jug. Allow the prunes to cool before splitting them and removing any stones. Butter a 1¾ pint pudding basin and line the basin with prunes, skin side out. Finely chop the remaining prunes and allow to fully cool. Put water on to boil for the pudding and cover the pan so that the water simmers, either with a trivet in the bottom or using a steamer saucepan with a basket. Cream together in a bowl, the butter, caster sugar and the rest of the lemon zest, then add the egg yolks, beating in carefully. Fold in the flour, to which you have added the baking powder, and also the breadcrumbs. Finally add the remaining chopped prunes. In a separate bowl whisk the egg whites until they stand in soft peaks and fold these into the mixture. Pour the mixture carefully into the prune-lined basin and then cover the top with a layer of buttered greaseproof paper and a second layer of foil, which is secured round the basin with string. Steam steadily for 1½ to 1¾ hours making sure that the pudding does not boil dry. When cooked, carefully run a knife round the inside of the basin and turn out onto a serving dish. Serve with the hot liquor. Ice cream, fresh cream, or custard can be additional accompaniments.

To make the sauce, mix the arrowroot with a little of the cooled prune liquor. Heat ¾ pint of the remaining liquor in a saucepan with the brown sugar, and add the arrowroot, bring to nearly boiling or until thickened, stirring continuously, allow to cool slightly and add the rum. Serve hot with the pudding.

Queen Mary's Pudding

This is a lovely pudding, especially if made with tart apples. It is very simple and quick to prepare, even if the cooking time is a little long.

INGREDIENTS

4 oz. plain flour   4 oz. white breadcrumbs   4 oz. suet   2 tbs. golden syrup   2 grated cooking apples
4 oz. raisins   1 tsp. baking powder   Milk to mix

METHOD

Combine all the ingredients in a large bowl adding enough milk to give a soft dropping consistency. Put in a large basin which has been well greased with butter. Cover with a layer of greased tin foil and secure tightly. Steam steadily for 4 hours making sure the pudding doesn't boil dry. Serve with a sweet sauce such as custard.

Malvern Fruit Pudding

Modern versions of Malvern Pudding are often more like a summer pudding. This is more of a traditional version with a light custard top. This pudding dates back to the kitchen of George III (born 1738, died 1820), and has remained popular ever since.

INGREDIENTS
**BASE: 3 oz. butter   2 lbs. prepared fruit, crisp cooking apples, or firm pears   4 oz. soft light brown sugar
3 oz. chopped walnuts   Zest of two lemons, and juice of one   ½ tsp. ground cinnamon
TOPPING: 2 oz. butter   2 oz. cornflour   1½ pints milk   2 large eggs   2 oz. caster sugar
2 oz. demarara sugar   ½ tsp. ground cinnamon**

METHOD
Filling: Pare, core and cut the fruit into medium sized chunks melt the butter in a large frying pan and lightly cook the fruit for about 10 minutes until it has softened, stir in the sugar, cinnamon, lemon zest and juice and the walnuts and gently cook for a further 2 minutes until all the ingredients are well combined. Do not let the walnuts burn. Arrange the fruit in a large oven-proof dish.

Topping: Mix a little of the milk into the cornflour and then bring the rest of the milk and caster sugar to the boil and then pour onto the cornflour paste stirring briskly as it thickens adding half the butter. Allow to cool a little and add the 2 eggs which have been beaten and strained. Add the cinnamon and whisk well into the mixture. Pour over the fruit mixture covering it completely. Sprinkle the demarara sugar over the custard topping and finally dot the remainder of the butter over the top. Put the dish under a hot grill and brown until it is bubbling and caramelised. Serve with ratafia or macaroon biscuits and eat immediately.

Catherine of Aragon's Seville Pudding

This pudding was a great favourite of Catherine of Aragon (born 1485, died 1536), and must have reminded her of home comforts with the combined flavours of the Seville oranges and Spanish wine.

INGREDIENTS
FOR THE SUNDAE: You will need a large buttered basin   4 oz. white breadcrumbs   2 oz. self-raising flour
2 oz. butter   2 oz. caster sugar   2 eggs   2 tbs. dark Seville marmalade
FOR THE SAUCE: Yolks of 2 large eggs   3 tbs. icing sugar   5 tbs. sweet sherry

METHOD
Mix all the ingredients together in a bowl and pour into the buttered basin. Cover with a sheet of greased tin foil and secure tightly over the pudding. Steam for 2 hours ensuring the pudding does not boil dry. Make the sherry sauce by putting all the ingredients into a basin stood over a bowl of simmering water. Whisk until thick, light and frothy. Serve pudding with the sherry sauce and whipped cream.

Queen Victoria's Brown Windsor Soup

Queen Victoria (born 1819, died 1901) was particularly fond of this hearty soup and consequently it made frequent appearances on the menus of state banquets. From the turn of the 19th century various manifestations of it could be found almost everywhere, from the corner-house cafés to the dining rooms of every railway station up and down the country! Sadly, many of these were greasy, lacklustre imitations of the original. Today, it has completely gone out of vogue, which·is a great pity because made properly, it is delicious.

INGREDIENTS

2 tbs. butter   4 oz. beef skirt   4 oz. mutton or lamb neck fillet   2.2 pints good beef stock   1 medium onion peeled and sliced
1 large carrot peeled and finely chopped   1 large parsnip peeled and finely chopped   2 heaped tbs. plain flour
1 bouquet garni, or freshly chopped herbs such as thyme, parsley, rosemary, and savoury   A large pinch of chilli powder
To serve quarter pint Madeira wine

METHOD

Trim most of the fat off the meat, and cut into ½ inch cubes. Toss cubes in the flour ensuring they are well coated. In a large heavy-based saucepan, melt the butter over a low heat so that it doesn't burn. Gently brown the meat cubes for about 5 minutes, add any left over flour and stir until the sauce is golden brown and thick. To this add the diced vegetables, stock and bouquet garni. Cover with a well-fitting lid, and then simmer very slowly for 2 to 3 hours.

Just before serving remove the bouquet garni, and stir in the Madeira wine, season to taste, and bring back to temperature without allowing it to boil. Serve this beautifully fragrant soup with croutons, or french bread.

Maids of Honour

These are more correctly known as Richmond Maids of Honour. Tradition has it that whilst strolling through Hampton Court, Henry VIII (born 1491, died 1547), came across Catherine of Aragon's maids of honour eating these little cakes. When the King tasted one he declared them to be delicious and asked what they were called. Since they were invented by Queen Catherine's pastry cook in the mid 1520s they had no official name. Henry, who was keen to impress Anne Boleyn amongst the Queen's attendants, immediately declared they be called Maids of Honour, and so the name stuck!

INGREDIENTS

8 oz. puff pastry (although I actually find shortcrust better behaved)   8 oz. curd or cottage cheese   3 oz. caster sugar
2 oz. currants   Grated zest of a lemon   Pinch mixed spice   ½ oz. blanched and finely chopped almonds   ½ oz. soft butter

METHOD

Pre-heat the oven to 375°F or gas 5. Rub cheese through a fine sieve into a mixing bowl, then add all the other filling ingredients. Mix well to a soft consistency. Roll out the pastry, cut into rounds and use to line 16 patty tins which have been greased. Half fill the pastry cases with the filling mixture. Bake in the centre of the oven for about 25 minutes until golden brown. Allow to cool for 5 minutes after cooking before very carefully removing from the tin and putting on a wire rack. When cool, sprinkle with a little icing sugar mixed with a little grated nutmeg.

Hampton Court Palace

Balmoral Girdle Scones

Queen Victoria (born 1819, died 1901), and Prince Albert both loved their Scottish home in Balmoral and doubtless enjoyed the opportunity to eat simpler fare occasionally. These girdle scones are very plain, quickly made, and quickly eaten.

INGREDIENTS

8 oz. plain flour   ½ level tsp. bicarbonate of soda   1 level tsp. cream of tartar   Pinch of salt
2 oz. butter   ¼ pint sour milk   Lard for greasing girdle

SMETHOD

Sift all the dry ingredients together, and rub in the butter finely. Make a well and pour in the soured milk, mixing the ingredients together to form a fairly stiff dough. Roll out very lightly on a floured board to ¼ inch thick. Heat the girdle or a heavy-based frying pan and grease very lightly. Bake the scones until golden brown and then flip over to cook the other side. Makes about 10. Can be served with sweet or savoury toppings and makes a lovely accompaniment to soup. These will keep in an airtight tin once cooled for 2 or 3 days.

King George VI and Queen Elizabeth's Gingerbread

This recipe was from René Roussin, Chef de Cuisine to the household of King George VI (born 1895, died 1952) and Queen Elizabeth, and gingerbread was a regular feature in the royal kitchen.

INGREDIENTS

12 oz. plain flour   Pinch of salt   1 rounded tsp. of ground ginger   1 tsp. bicarbonate of soda   1 tsp. of baking powder
2 oz. chopped preserved ginger   6 oz. soft brown sugar   5 oz. butter   4 oz. black treacle   4 oz. golden syrup
1 egg   ⅓ pint milk

METHOD

Pre-heat oven to 160°C or gas mark 3. Sift all the dry ingredients together, stir in chopped preserved ginger. In a saucepan warm the butter, sugar, treacle and syrup until they have melted together, but do not let them get hot. Add the milk just to warm it, and stir together. Beat the egg into the warm liquid ingredients and pour into the dry ingredients. Mix to a soft consistency and pour into an 8 inch square tin which has been well greased or lined with baking paper. Bake in the middle of the oven for 1½ hours. Turn onto a wire rack to cool. Cut into squares when cold and serve.

Queen Victoria's Shortbread

This shortbread was from celebrated master chef, Swiss-born Gabriel Tschumi who served three monarchs, Queen Victoria, Edward VII and George V. Known throughout the royal households as "Chummy", his 'reign' spanned forty years, and on his retirement he was awarded the Royal Victorian Medal, in recognition of his achievement. This shortbread recipe was the favourite of Queen Victoria (born 1819, died 1901), and she was reputed to have eaten a little of it every day.

INGREDIENTS
12 oz. plain flour   8 oz. butter   4 oz. caster sugar   Lightly buttered baking tray

METHOD
Pre-heat oven. Rub in butter and sugar in a bowl and then work in flour lightly using only the finger tips. Roll out very thinly on a lightly dusted surface to about ⅛ inch thick, cut into rounds, prick with a fork and bake on a buttered baking tray in a moderate oven 310°F or gas mark 3, for about 15 minutes until a pale golden brown. Cool on a wire rack. Sprinkle with a little sugar and eat when completely cool. Will keep in an airtight tin for 5 days.

Queen Mary's Cheese Biscuits

These are so easy to make and keep well in an airtight tin. They are delicious with all cheeses, and make a lovely gift instead of the ubiquitous bottle of wine if you are invited out for a meal.

INGREDIENTS
4 oz. grated fresh Parmesan cheese   4 oz. butter   4 oz. plain flour

METHOD
Mix to a paste on a board. Roll out very thinly an eighth of an inch. Cut into rounds, ovals, and squares. Bake on a greased tray in a medium oven 310°F or gas mark 3 for about 20 minutes until crisp and pale golden brown. Sandwich together with a choice of the following fillings.

Fillings for the above biscuits: Sandwich Palais Royale; two biscuits joined together with smoked haddock and butter purée.

York filling: two biscuits joined together with anchovy or sardine purée.

Tortelettes Windsor: Two biscuits joined together with a filling of cheese, finely minced ham and bechamel sauce.

Crêpes Suzette

This recipe was made famous by Henri Charpentier, a celebrity chef of his day who cooked in many esteemed establishments and who prepared dishes for most of the crowned heads and dignitaries of Europe and America. On this occasion he was preparing a dessert for the future King Edward VII (born 1841, died 1910), and the sauce was accidentally burned. Charpentier remedied the situation by renaming the dish immediately Crêpes Princesse. The Prince, delighted by this dish, and noticing that there was only one lady present amongst 18 gentlemen diners, immediately requested the dish be renamed in her honour, and so Crêpes Suzette was born. The next day by way of thanks, Charpentier received from the Prince a jewelled ring, a Panama hat and a cane!

INGREDIENTS

FOR THE PANCAKES: 2 eggs   1½ **tbs. milk**   1½ **tbs. plain flour**   **A pinch of salt**
1 dessert spoon of water   **2 tbs. clarified butter**
FOR THE SAUCE: 4 oz. butter   **1 tbs. vanilla caster sugar**
2 fl.oz. each of maraschino, curaçao and kirschwasser pre-mixed and divided between two small jugs
1 tsp. lemon zest   **1 tsp. orange zest**

METHOD

For the pancakes: Beat together all the ingredients except the butter, to form a smooth thin cream. Melt the butter in a frying pan or skillet, until very hot, when it bubbles pour in enough batter to thinly cover the bottom of the pan. Keep moving the pan. After a minute turn pancake over with a spatula and just cook the other side. Quickly fold the pancake in half and then quarters so it becomes a triangle. Set aside in a warm place and repeat process to make four pancakes.

This sauce can be made in advance as it keeps in a sealed jar in the fridge without spoiling. To make it, add the vanilla sugar to the zest of both orange and lemon, cover and leave for a day or two. CAUTION: BE EXTREMELY CAREFUL MAKING THE SAUCE AS IT WILL IGNITE IN THE FRYING PAN. Melt the butter in a saucepan and when it begins to bubble add one of the jugs of combined spirit. It should immediately catch alight, if not you can light it with a long taper. As the fire goes out add the sugar and zest. Plunge the pancakes into the boiling sauce and add the rest of the spirit. It will re-ignite, and when the flames die down they are ready to serve. Serve with freshly whipped cream.

Forty-Three

Queen Anne's Pudding

Queen Anne (born 1665, died 1714), was the last English monarch to have eaten with her fingers; since this dessert has always been attributed to her, I can only think she must have made an exception with puddings and at least used a spoon!

INGREDIENTS

4 oz. white breadcrumbs   1 pint whole milk   3 oz. caster sugar   1 oz. granulated sugar   1 oz. butter
Zest of a small lemon   3 eggs   4 tbs. jam

METHOD

Butter a deep 1½ pint pie dish and pre-heat the oven to 310°F, or gas mark 3. Mix together the lemon zest, granulated sugar and breadcrumbs in a basin. In a saucepan warm the milk and add the butter allowing it to melt. Separate the eggs putting the whites into a spotlessly clean bowl. Add the yolks to the warm milk and mix before pouring onto the breadcrumbs. Allow to stand for half an hour.

Spread the breadcrumb mixture into the dish and bake for half an hour until firm and set. Take from the oven and spread with jam. Whisk the egg whites until the mix stands in stiff peaks. Gently fold in the caster sugar with a large spoon or spatula. Cover the pie dish with whirls of meringue, returning the dish to the oven and baking for a further 30 to 40 minutes until the meringue is crisp and pale gold. Serve immediately with whipped cream.

The Queen's House, Greenwich Palace, London

Queen Elizabeth's Date & Walnut Cake

I believe this was one of the favourite cakes of Queen Elizabeth, the Queen Mother (born 1900, died 2002), and is very quick and easy to make. It has a lovely soft and slightly chewy texture from soaking the dates.

INGREDIENTS
**8 oz. stoned chopped dates   1 cup of boiling water   1 tsp. bicarbonate of soda   3 oz. butter   10 oz. plain flour
1 tsp. baking powder   ½ tsp. salt   8 oz. light soft brown sugar   2 oz. chopped walnuts   1 beaten egg
1 tsp. vanilla essence
TOPPING: 5 tbs. light soft brown sugar   2 oz. butter   2 tbs. cream**

METHOD
Pre-heat the oven to 310°F or gas mark 4. Grease or line a baking tin 10 inches square. Pour the boiling water into a basin with the dates and add the bicarbonate of soda, stir in and leave to stand for half an hour. Meanwhile, combine the salt, baking powder and flour and rub the butter into it finely. Add the sugar, chopped walnuts, vanilla and egg, and then drain the dates and stir everything in together. Place mixture into the baking tin and put in the oven to cook for about 35 minutes. To make the topping, put all the ingredients into a saucepan and boil gently for 3 minutes. When the cake is cool, spread the topping over and sprinkle with more chopped walnuts if required.

George VI's Favourite Savoury

Roussin prepared this simple dish which was much enjoyed by King George VI (born 1895, died 1952).

INGREDIENTS
Rounds of white bread cut ¼ of an inch thick   **Slices of gruyère cheese**
Thin slices of cooked ham   **Melted butter and cooking oil**

METHOD
Layer the first round of bread with a slice of cheese, place the ham on top then a further layer of cheese, and finally the last slice of bread. Heat the butter and oil together in a frying pan and cook each side until the cheese just melts. Turn the sandwich over and repeat with the other side. Drain and serve immediately.

METRIC CONVERSIONS

The weights, measures and oven temperatures used in the preceding recipes can be easily converted to their metric equivalents. The conversions listed below are only approximate, having been rounded up or down as may be appropriate.

Weights

Avoirdupois	Metric
1 oz.	just under 30 grams
4 oz. (¼ lb.)	app. 115 grams
8 oz. (½ lb.)	app. 230 grams
1 lb.	454 grams

Liquid Measures

Imperial	Metric
1 tablespoon (liquid only)	20 millilitres
1 fl. oz.	app. 30 millilitres
1 gill (¼ pt.)	app. 145 millilitres
½ pt.	app. 285 millilitres
1 pt.	app. 570 millilitres
1 qt.	app. 1.140 litres

Oven Temperatures

	°Fahrenheit	Gas Mark	°Celsius
Slow	300	2	150
	325	3	170
Moderate	350	4	180
	375	5	190
	400	6	200
Hot	425	7	220
	450	8	230
	475	9	240

Flour as specified in these recipes refers to plain flour unless otherwise described.